The Open University

Arts: A Second Level Course
Seventeenth-century England: A Changing Culture, 1618–1689

The Development of Prose

Prepared for the course team by Joan Bellamy and Simon Eliot

The Open University Press

Cover illustrations

Front Detail from 'England and Ireland's sad theatre, or William Laud, heretofore Archbishop of Canterbury, his trance and vision. Wherein is laid open before us the miserable cruelties and unheard of tyrannies caused by the Popish factions.', 10 January 1645. (British Museum, Department of Prints and Drawings. Photo: John R. Freeman.)

Back Engraved title page from John Donne's *LXXX Sermons*, 1640. Engraving by M. Merian. (Bodleian Library, Oxford. Fol. 328.)

The Open University Press
Walton Hall, Milton Keynes
MK7 6AA

First published 1981. Reprinted 1984.

Designed by the Graphic Design Group of the Open University.

Printed in Great Britain by Eyre & Spottiswoode Limited at Grosvenor Press, Portsmouth.

ISBN 0 335 11047 9

This text forms part of an Open University course. The complete list of the course appears at the end of this text.

For general availability of supporting material referred to in this text, please write to Open University Educational Enterprises Limited, 12 Cofferidge Close, Stony Stratford, Milton Keynes, MK11 1BY, Great Britain.

Further information on Open University courses may be obtained from the Admissions Office, The Open University, PO Box 48, Walton Hall, Milton Keynes, MK7 6AB.

1.2

The Development of Prose

Contents

Introduction

In this study of the changes that took place in the prose of the seventeenth century we shall be looking at examples from many different kinds of writing, including published sermons, pamphlets, histories, philosophy, science and political science, as well as from more conventional literary works. You will meet here, among others, writers such as Bacon, Hobbes, Winstanley and Dryden who are discussed in other parts of the course but in a different context. We hope your study of them here as stylists and in the light of the development of prose will offer a different but important dimension to your general understanding of them.

We have had a difficult problem in deciding which authors to study out of the enormous range of possibilities and we have not been able to present anything like the complete picture of prose writing in the seventeenth century. As a way of coping with the diversity of prose styles, we have adopted two different but complementary approaches. In sections 1 and 3 Simon Eliot gives a broad historical survey of changes in prose style during the period, while in section 2 Joan Bellamy looks in detail at a number of political pamphlets of the sixteen-thirties and sixteen-forties. We believe that by adopting such an approach we have been able to indicate the main aspects of change in seventeenth-century prose, what some of the factors were that brought about such changes and how, by the end of the century, the features of modern English writing had come into being.

As you consider the changes in prose, remember that you are meeting not with some abstract model of a seventeenth-century writer – there can be no such thing – nor should you try to squeeze the writer into a rigid model of a steady, overall predictable progression and development. Each example of prose here is inevitably the work of a highly individual man, with a specific way of looking at life, with a special aim in writing what he does and with a way of using language which may be as distinctive as peoples' personalities are.

You should try to use this booklet in parallel with the course as a whole, coming back to it from time to time as you work through the other material. Remember also that while we have had to be highly selective here, there are many other examples of seventeenth-century prose in the Anthology and on the cassettes, as well as relevant discussions in the blocks (for example, Block 4, *The Revolution and its Impact,* and Block 5, *Political Ideas,* have important background material for Section 2, 'Opposition Pamphlets').

Set book

You will need the following set book as you work through *The Development of Prose:*

Ann Hughes (ed.) (1980) *Seventeenth Century England: A Changing Culture,* Volume 1, *Primary Sources,* Ward Lock (referred to as the Anthology).

Cassette

Cassette 3 (AC207) contains readings of seventeenth-century prose which have been selected to illustrate the developments which are discussed in this booklet. You will find it valuable, therefore. to listen to the cassette and read its associated notes as you work on *The Development of Prose.*

1 Early Seventeenth-century Prose

I would like you to start by reading the following three sentences:

> *Julius Caesar* (for whom, and of the Roman Free State, more than what appertains, is not here to be discours'd) having subdu'd most parts of Gallia, which by a potent faction, he had obtain'd of the Senat as his Province for many years, stirr'd up with a desire of adding still more glory to his name, and the whole Roman Empire to his ambition, som say, with a farr meaner and ignobler, the desire of Brittish Pearls, whose bigness he delighted to ballance in his hand, *determins,* and that upon no unjust pretended occasion, *to trie his Force in the conquest also of Britain.* [Italics added.]
>
>

John Milton (1670)

> A cold comming they had of it, at this time of the yeare; just, the worst time of the yeare, to take a journey, and specially a long journey, in.
>
>

Lancelot Andrewes (1622)

> The ill effects of this superfluity of talking have already over-whelmed most other arts and professions; insomuch, that when I consider the means of happy living, and the causes of their corruption, I can hardly forbear recanting what I said before; and concluding, that eloquence ought to be banished out of all civil societies, as a thing fatal to peace and good manners.
>
>

Thomas Sprat (1667)

All three sentences represented perfectly acceptable ways of writing prose in their time. How is it that such different forms of prose could be written within fifty years of each other (at a time when most things changed slowly) and why is it that, while the first two seem alien to us, the movement of the last seems so familiar?

Throughout the sixteenth century there had been a great literary struggle between those who thought that any learned or important book should be written in Latin and those who believed that such works should be in English. Although English was in the ascendancy by 1600, many writers had the uncomfortable feeling that something had been lost with the decline of Latin. It occurred to many that one way of keeping the best of both languages would be to write English as though it were Latin – that is, by basing their English prose styles on those of classical authors. Now this presented them with a problem, because Latin was an inflected language, while, by the late sixteenth century anyway, English was almost totally uninflected. By 'inflected' I mean that in Latin the endings of many words are changed according to the job that they do in a particular sentence. It is therefore possible in Latin to arrange the words of a sentence in different ways without degrading the meaning. Now in English this is not true. Very few words change their endings when their job changes in a sentence, so the *order* in which the words come is very important. Change the word order of an English sentence and you will very likely change its meaning. The longer or more complicated a sentence is, the more vital it is that the reader keep a firm grip on all its constituent parts. If he does not, then he will lose his way in the sentence and thus lose the sentence's meaning.

Late Renaissance writers of English prose who wished to model their style on a Latin author therefore faced the problem that the complicated Latin sentence, if translated literally, does not make much sense in English. How can you write most sentences in English following the common Latin practice of putting the verb either at the end or near it?

The problem was greater for late sixteenth-century and early seventeenth-century writers than merely a matter of word order. The Latin author most admired by English writers of this period was Marcus Tullius Cicero (106–43 BC), whose style was characterized by very long sentences in which there is often one main clause, surrounded by a multitude of balancing clauses and phrases which clarify and modify it. To over-simplify, the Ciceronian sentence is constructed something like this:

subject then *qualifying clauses* then *object* then *verb*.

Even if a writer acknowledged that in order to write English at all, it was necessary to conform to the normal order of subject, verb, object, it was still possible to produce a sentence like the first quoted on page 5. (I have italicized the main clause to show where it occurs.) This sort of sentence was known as the *periodic* and it is a particular characteristic, though rarely in such an extreme form, of Ciceronian style. (Milton was unusual in that he was still writing periodic sentences as late as the sixteen-seventies. For another example of Ciceronian style and the sense of grandeur it could create, look at the first sentence of *Paradise Lost*.) There was, however, a great danger in the Ciceronian sentence: the writer might be tempted to pile qualifying phrase upon phrase, not because it added to and developed the meaning, but because it was a good way of adding 'weight' and dignity to what he said.

It is not surprising that Francis Bacon, a revolutionary in style as much as in scientific method, reacted so strongly against Ciceronian prose. He surveyed the learning and language of the early Renaissance and found it pedantic, muddled and petty: '. . . men began to hunt more after words than matter; and more after the choiceness of the phrase, and the round and clean composition of the sentence.' (*Advancement of Learning,* page 26.) If human knowledge was to be put on a proper footing, he argued, it would have to be expressed clearly in unaffected, straightforward prose.

EXERCISE

Why is Bacon making such a fuss? Isn't the Ciceronian sentence just a matter of taste, you either like it or you don't; you either add decoration, or you decide to leave your sentences plain? How would you answer such a criticism of Bacon?

DISCUSSION

I do not think style is just a matter of decoration. Style affects the whole structure of the sentence and therefore influences the meaning of every word placed in that sentence.

This was certainly true of Bacon. He regarded words and the styles which in part determined their use with deep suspicion. Words could so easily become traps or double-edged swords which could be as dangerous to the writer as to the reader:

> . . . although we think we govern our words, . . . yet certain it is that words, as a Tartar's bow, do shoot back upon the understanding of the wisest, and mightily entangle and pervert the judgement; so as it is almost necessary in all controversies and disputations, to imitate the wisdom of the mathmeticians, in setting down in the very beginning the definitions of our words and terms . . .

> (*Advancement of Learning,* page 128.)

For Bacon the ideal was a simple, unambiguous language in which each word stood for a specific and precise 'thing', rather in the same way that a mathematical symbol does.

In fact, like most Renaissance thinkers, Bacon was not being as revolutionary as he appeared. Although he seems to be encouraging a new English prose style, that style was in fact derived from another classical author, Lucius Annaeus Seneca (c. 5 BC–AD 65). In many ways Seneca's style was the opposite of Cicero's: it encouraged short sentences, often consisting of just one main clause. When Seneca wrote longer sentences these tended to be co-ordinated, that is a series of main clauses tacked together by simple conjunctions ('and', 'but', etc.), rather than a main clause with a lot of subordinate clauses related to it (linked by 'which', 'that', etc.). The effect of Ciceronian sentences was of a slow, smooth, stately, progression to a known end – such a style implied a stable set of values which were unchanging and secure. Seneca's style created the opposite effect. The short sentences produced a jerky, clipped, laconic style. The Ciceronian sentence is clearly the product of a mind which has a completed thought to express. The Senecan sentence provides a picture of a mind thinking as it goes along.

Often associated with Seneca as the parent of this 'curt' style was the Roman historian, Tacitus (c. 55–120 AD). Like Seneca, Tacitus employed short simple or co-ordinated sentences, but he took this style further, packing his short sentences with meaning, thus creating a terse, aphoristic prose in which individual words work very hard for their living.

EXERCISE

In what ways would a prose style based on Seneca and Tacitus appeal to the author of the *Advancement of Learning*?

DISCUSSION

Because it would seem to get rid of the over-elaborate, the 'more words than the matter' type of periodic sentence. The 'curt' style forced fewer words to work harder and seemed to promise a closer approximation of 'words' to 'things'.

I use the word 'seem' because, by 1623, when Bacon rewrote, significantly in Latin, the *Advancement of Learning* as *De Augmentis Scientiarum*, the curt style, which he had thought promised so much, was included, along with Ciceronian prose, as just another 'vanity of study'.

Bacon shifted away from the curt style because it was as open to abuse as Ciceronian prose. To condense thought too much is dangerous because such condensing can result in obscurity. The aphoristic style of Tacitus has an additional danger: difficult points can be made to appear easy by short, sharp, 'witty' epigrams.

Worried by this, Bacon rewrote some of his essays (originally printed in 1597) in 1625 in a less curt style. Compare these versions of the same passage from *Of Studies*.

1597	*1625*
Studies serve for pastimes, for ornaments and for abilities. Their chiefe use for pastime is in privatenes and retiring; for ornamente is in discourse, and for abilitie is in judgement. For expert men can execute, but learned men are fittest to judge or censure.	Studies serve for Delight, for ornament, and for ability. Their chief use for delight, is in privatenes and retiring; for ornament, is in Discourse; and for ability, is in the judgement and disposition of business. For expert men can execute, and perhaps judge of particulars, one by one; but the generall counsels, and the plots, and marshalling of affairs, come best from those that are learned.

The final sentence in the 1625 version is neither Ciceronian nor 'curt'. It is in fact closer to what contemporaries were beginning to call the 'loose' style. In the 'loose' style:

1   there's no obligation on sentences to be predominantly long or short, 'loose' prose is often a mixture of the two;

2   the structure of each sentence is not dependent on a tight-knit system of main and subordinate clauses locked together, rather it is a loose assemblage of simple sentences.

Such a style also claimed, quite legitimately, parentage from Seneca and Tacitus, for when not writing concisely, both Latin authors used this alternative, freer mode. Indeed, their styles were a mixture of the two modes. We shouldn't think of 'curt' and 'loose' as being totally separate. All English imitators of these styles mixed the two, though in different proportions.

But Bacon's objections to the curt style came too late, for by 1623 it was well established. The loose style, too, was becoming more common, though it would be wrong to suggest that its popularity was simply due to Bacon's influence.

EXERCISE

Apart from Bacon's original encouragement of the curt and, later, of the loose style, can you think of any reason for them being preferred to Ciceronian prose? Look again at the quotation from Milton and compare it with the excerpt from Bacon's essays.

DISCUSSION

Relatively short sentences and sentences without too much subordination are easier to read and understand in a non-inflected language like English. In the 'loose' Senecan sentence you do not have to wait for the final word, as you would in a Ciceronian sentence, to make sense of what is being said. Senecan and related styles simply fit English better.

The mood of the time also had something to do with the use of Senecan prose. The older certainties and stabilities of the Renaissance, so well expressed by the slow, elaborate confidence of the Ciceronian sentence (it knew where it was going!), no longer applied in the Jacobean period. Things had lost their certainty. A style which, in its jerky hesitant manner, was able to dash off in a new direction at every conjunction, would match the new instability well, and would clearly have an advantage over the Ciceronian dinosaur.

EXERCISE

Let's get down to a longer example. Read the excerpt from the sermon *Of the Nativity* by Lancelot Andrewes (1555–1626) in the Anthology (extract 125). Is this Ciceronian or Senecan prose?

DISCUSSION

With its use of short, sharp, simple sentences, with very little subordination, Andrewes's prose is an example of the Senecan 'curt' style. There is a chopped, urgent, breathless quality about the writing which would have been impossible in a Ciceronian periodic sentence.

For the Protestant Andrewes, God revealed himself not in miracles or saints' lives but through the language of the Bible, particularly the language of the Latin Vulgate text. For Andrewes, the closer you attended to the text the closer and clearer God became.

In the hands of a preacher less successful than Andrewes this 'crumbling of the text', as a contemporary image describes it, could become a dry and pedantic exercise. In Andrewes's sermons the meticulous analysis of words is accompanied by a vivid imagination and a deep sense of moral drama.

At the beginning of his sermon, in a passage which is not printed in the Anthology, Andrewes observes that the qualities are paired, not like with like, but with their potential opposite. Mercy and truth are often at odds, and righteousness (justice) and peace are not easy bed-fellows. He then asserts

Figure 1 Portrait of Lancelot Andrewes by unknown artist. (Bodleian Library, Oxford.)

that the four principles were broken asunder by Adam's fall, and come together again in Christ at Christ's birth. Andrewes is therefore arguing that the reconciling or 'meeting' of these four principles is a unique feature of Christianity. Thus the excerpt you have just read is having to do two jobs at once. The main one is to dramatize the radical differences between these four qualities, and the second is to hint at the astonishing power of Christianity to fuse these opposing forces. This is no idle intellectual game for Andrewes. On this reconciliation depends the salvation of the soul, so his pursuit of the truth of this through the word of God is relentless. This urgency is well expressed by the image, 'our salvation lies a bleeding, all this while'. There is a race against time and yet it cannot be hurried, that is made clear by the legal image which suggests a long, slow struggle between justice and mercy which cannot and will not be hurried. It also shows how uncertain our fate is: 'we stand . . . and know not what shall become of us'. The personifications of the original psalm are developed through this legal metaphor, and peace and mercy (now more appropriately paired by Andrews) become the defence council, truth and righteousness the prosecution. These are almost equally balanced, except that truth and righteousness, being absolutes, are 'more stiff'.

Do you see how rigorous Andrewes is being? He will not simplify or make things rhetorically easy by saying that the forces were precisely balanced. His determination to get the full meaning out of a word like

9

'righteousness' will not allow him to make generalizations. Truth and righteousness *are* more difficult to reconcile with the possibility of salvation, and righteousness more difficult than truth.

As though responding to the intractable nature of righteousness, Andrewes's argument concentrates more and more exclusively on that quality rather than the other three, finally pinning down the nature of that intractability as a demand for 'satisfaction'. But, though the prose concentrates on the obstruction, it does not let us forget the final goal to which Andrewes is driving – that of a reconciliation or 'meeting'. Notice how many times 'meet' or 'meeting' crop up in the passage. It is like a motif in music recurring again and again. Such a motif is particularly necessary to bind together a prose which, with its lively but fragmented Senecan form, seems to move with breathless speed from one idea to the next.

Having worried the idea of 'satisfaction' out of righteousness, Andrewes's argument can broaden out again to take in all four qualities once more. In the third paragraph from the end of the extract he picks up the word 'meet' and at last specifies the sort of meeting he is talking about: 'not to meet and argue . . . but to meet, and kiss'. This is a signal to abandon the legal image ('meet and argue') and offer an image of a creative reconciliation – harmony: 'how to set a song of these four parts, in good harmony'. The final paragraph of the extract links the new idea of harmony with the text on which his sermon is based (it is after all a psalm and meant to be sung).

EXERCISE

Do you notice anything striking about the final paragraph?

DISCUSSION

It is almost in the form of a logical argument. The short sentences take on the form of premises and conclusions. The urgent argument has given way, for the time being, to solid, unadorned conviction.

In other preachers such a dogmatic assertion might be suspect, appearing like an attempt to bully the congregation into faith, but in Andrewes the final assertions seem well-rooted in an exhaustive exploration of the text and a relentless determination to do full justice to each word of it.

Although in some ways Andrewes's style is very idiosyncratic, it remains essentially impersonal, unlike another preacher equally, though differently, influenced by the curt and loose styles – John Donne (1572–1631).

EXERCISE

Please read the second excerpt from Donne in your Anthology (extract 126b). Can you see any ways in which this differs from the Andrewes passage in form or content?

DISCUSSION

The first thing that strikes me is the difference in sentence length. Gone are the curt sentences of Andrewes and in their place are sentences just as long as those found in Milton; but they are different from Milton's. You don't have to wait for the end of the sentence to understand the meaning of Donne's loose prose; that's rather fortunate since this passage consists of just two huge sentences!

The other thing that strikes me is the tone – it is very personal. There is a constant harping on 'I' and 'me' and 'mine', quite unlike Andrewes's impersonal preoccupation with the text. (See Block 2, pages 72–3, for a discussion of the personal tone in Donne's poetry.) Donne seems to take the time to expand his meaning by explaining it through one image and then repeating the point by playing variations on that image. Thus in the first sentence we have the image of Donne being thrown into a debtors' prison in order to repay the debts of his youth, followed immediately by a reworking of that idea in another image: Donne fading away in a hospital ('spital') paying the penalty of venereal disease. The link between these two images is emphasized by the choice of language – can you see how?

The prison is described by three adjectives – 'discomfortable', 'unwholesome', 'penurious'. The diseases are described by another triplet of adjectives – 'sharp', 'foul', 'infamous'. The

'recompense the wastefulness of my youth, with the beggary of mine age'

is balanced by

'recompense the wantoness of my youth, with that loathsomeness in mine age'.

Reading Donne is like listening to a virtuoso musician displaying his abilities by playing variation after variation on a theme:

'God shall deject, and impoverish, and evacuate that spirit.'

'God shall shake and enfeeble and enervate, destroy and demolish that constancy.'

Here it's a pattern of verbs rather than adjectives, and the pattern is not quite symmetrical (nor should it be – Donne, after all, is talking about the destruction of 'constancy'.). Later the double image of debt and sickness returns, this time reversed:

'I shall lay hold upon riches to succour me, and comfort me in my sickness. . .'

'I shall snatch after favour, and good opinion, to comfort me in my poverty . . .'

This elaboration of ideas through verbal patterns reaches a grand climax in the last line of the excerpt which ends with four heavy, resounding adverbs like the tolling of a knell. As all four adverbs begin with the prefix 'irre' and are rather similar (particularly the middle two), the reader has to take them slowly, thus allowing their full force to come through. It is quite likely too that, for a seventeenth-century audience at least, there would be an additional strand of meaning running through these last four words. The 'irre' prefix is remarkably close to Latin 'irae', as in the phrase 'dies irae', the day of wrath, of God's final judgement of Man.

Did you notice that Donne has been building up the reader's concentration for this moment of crisis by repeating the word 'when' no less than eight times in the massive second sentence? Did you notice too that, although throughout the rest of the passage Donne uses the personal pronoun 'I', he substitutes this in the last two lines with 'we'? From being observers of another man's anguish, we have become, by the simplest change in grammar, his fellow sufferers.

2 Opposition Pamphlets

In this section we are going to look at a few examples of opposition pamphlets which appeared between 1633 and 1652. This kind of 'shirt-sleeve' writing rarely if ever appears in literary anthologies, though our understanding of its importance is growing. It was certainly part of the process of change towards simpler, more flexible and 'modern' prose style which we are trying to trace.

The pamphlets are more than just 'influences' though, they are interesting in their own right, both for their stylistic qualities and because they speak directly to us, giving the flavour of the controversies and conflicts that marked the deepening tensions and crises of the time. They were part of the serious and dangerous business of influencing public opinion and moving people to political action.

In London in the first half of the seventeenth century the population was growing rapidly and the authorities were very sensitive to hostile propaganda and the possibility of riots. The opposition, successively to the bishops, to the King, and to the Presbyterians, pressed for more rights, including freedom of access to those powerful means of persuasion, the pulpit and the press. During the sixteen-thirties the government of Charles I enforced strict control over the press. The Stationer's Company was responsible for the good behaviour of its members whose numbers were restricted, while printers were subject to heavy fines for breaking regulations. The output of pamphlets rose nevertheless (see in Block 4, *The Revolution and its Impact,* the essay on *Areopagitica* and *C of R,* pages 149–50). The abolition in 1641 of the Star Chamber, which had heard trials for violating printing regulations, gave a stimulus to an even greater output of pamphlet literature. Parliament attempted to stem the tide in 1644 by seeking to reimpose controls, and it was against this that Milton was protesting in *Areopagitica.* Though censorship was back again in the sixteen-fifties, it was the Restoration which saw the revival of really strict surveillance. The censors were Roger L'Estrange and John Berkenhead, mocked by Andrew Marvell in *The Rehearsal Transpros'd* (see Block 7, *Milton and Marvell,* for a discussion of Marvell). For the first time ever a printer was hanged for illegal printing, after a trial brutally conducted by Lord Chief Justice Hyde, with L'Estrange as chief witness. As a warning to others the mutilated body of the offender was quartered and the parts set up on the gates of the City of London.

From the sixteen-thirties the influence of the press and pulpit grew in spite of bitter opposition and harassment, (*C of R,* pages 82–3). Though the growing readership of the press comprised widely differing levels of literacy and education, there were nevertheless important elements of a common culture, especially in religion, which writers could assume in their readers whether, like Milton, they were addressing an influential and learned audience, or like John Bastwick, a more plebeian one.

Most writers rested their arguments on the Authorized Version of the Bible as the divinely inspired source of truth. They echoed its style, language, images, and rhythms, harnessing those complex feelings which it inspires in audiences, even in present times. The sermon, too, was a strong influence on their style, which combined the religious and aesthetic authority of the Bible with the forms of classical rhetoric, the art of persuasive eloquence. Those aiming at a wider audience also adapted the dramatic devices of the theatre, the language of ballads and broadsheets and of popular idiom, thus helping to create forms of prose approximating more closely to ordinary speech – simpler, more flexible than before, more like the prose of today. We have no evidence that popular propagandists were seeking consciously to reform the language, though some, like Winstanley and the Levellers, demanded the use of the vernacular in all writings, including the law, as part of their resistance to any manifestations of 'the Norman yoke'.

Theirs is then the prose not of more conventional literature, but of persuasion and mobilization directed at a popular readership.

One of the most prolific of pamphlet writers was William Prynne (1600–69) a graduate of Oriel College, Oxford and a lawyer of Lincoln's Inn. His long work *Histriomastix* (1633), meaning 'a whip or scourge for actors', was as much an attack on the Court as on the theatre. He had already earned notoriety with a pamphlet *The Unloveliness of Love-Locks* (note the word-play!), attacking men who grew their hair long as effeminate and degenerate. He was also a scourge of the bishops, and *Histriomastix* provided Laud with an opportunity for silencing him.

The work attacked the theatre as a corrupter of morals which made vice attractive and tempted people to squander their money in loose living. Prynne was appalled at the idea of women acting and dancing on stage and refers specifically to some women actors who, 'In imitation of these some French women, or monsters rather on Michaelmas term 1629 attempted to act a French play, at the Playhouse in Blackfriars; an impudent, shameful, unwomanish, graceless if not more than whorish attempt' (page 414).

EXERCISE

Read the following passages from *Histriomastix* carefully and first try to decide why the book could be taken as a seditious attack on the Court; then describe the style of the passages and the method of argument.

Histriomastix

What shall I record the severally abominable adulteries of Venus; the infinite superlative incests, rapes, fornications, love-pranks, Sodomies, murders, cheats, with other such execrable wickednesses of Jupiter, the very worst, though greatest of the pagan deities? What shall I relate the several beastly flagitious practices, ceremonies, obscenities, of Juno, Bacchus, Cupid, Priapus, Mars, Serapis, Atys, Flora, the mother of the gods, or of the rest of that infernal crew, which come so frequent on our theatres? Is it not their filthiness, their lewdness so barbarously, so stupendously impious, that it even strikes men's hearts and tongues with horror, forbidding them to relate it?

(page 92)

Thus far the Waldenses and Albigenses, whose words I would the dancing, wanton (that I say not whorish) Herodiases, the effeminate sinqua-pace Caranto-frisking gallants of our age, together with our rustic hobbling satyrs, nymphs and dancing fairies who spend their strength, their time (especially the Easter, Whitsun, Midsummer and Christmas season) in lewd lascivious dancing, would now seriously consider.

(page 232)

. . . the daughter of Herodias entering in danced, and cut off the head of John the Baptist; and so she obtained the subterraneous places of Hell instead of an inheritance. Wherefore those who love rounds and dances have certainly a portion with her in Hell. A terrible sentence sufficient to startle all our dancing dames and frisking effeminate gallants, who make dancing their only excellence and supreme delight.

(page 260)

Trebellius Pollio relates that Martianus, Heraclianus, and Claudius, three worthy Romans, conspired together to murder Gallienus the Emperor (a man much besotted and taken up with plays, to which he likewise drew the magistrates and people by his lewd example), as

Flavius and others conspired Nero his murder too for the self-same cause, least the Commonweal being longer addicted to the circus and the theatre, should utterly perish through the allurements of pleasures; which murder they accomplished.

(page 465)

But there is no hope to see plays forbidden by the magistrates, for commonly they are the first at them. Thus far these foreigners. To pass by Cardus Sigonius, who enumerates the frequenting, tolerating and countenancing of stage-plays both by prince and people, as the inevitable forerunner, and chief occasion both of the destruction and overthrow of the Roman Empire by the Goths and Vandals.

(pages 484–5)

Women actors, notorious whores.
Dancing . . . Delight and skill in dancing, a badge of lewd, lascivious women and strumpets.

(The Table; i.e. 'index')

DISCUSSION

Laud persuaded the King that the references to Herodias, to French actresses and to women dancing were pointed at the Queen, herself French, who, as we know, was an enthusiastic participant in masques. The references to conspiracies and murders of rulers who patronized drama were taken as an incitement to readers to do the same to Charles I, who was himself fond of theatricals.

Argument by analogy was an important aspect of rhetoric and this is part of Prynne's method here. He draws authority for his case from precedents from the scriptures and from the Church fathers. Not only does he pile up one example after another, but he bludgeons us too with long lists of words as if he thinks sheer quantity of statement and description constitutes proof. Over-insistent he may be, but he relishes the sounds of words, and you may have listed one aspect of his style as carrying repetition of sounds: in words like filth*iness,* lewd*ness,* barbarou*sly,* stupendou*sly;* or *l*ewd *l*ascivious *d*ancing *d*ames; *ef*feminate *fr*isking. The rhetorical questions in the first quotation are characteristic of speechmaking. Notice how, having given us what one might reasonably take to be a well nigh exhaustive list of horrible crimes, he suggests that they are really too horrible to enumerate! You might also have noticed the antithesis in 'Jupiter, the very worst, though greatest, of the pagan deities' – another device of rhetoric. Note that he addresses his audience directly – 'What shall *I* record . . .?' – as if he is speaking to us. This helps, too, to explain the repetitions, the lists of synonyms, the numerous examples. Even the least attentive 'listener' could hardly fail to get the drift of the case at some point or another.

For writing *Histriomastix* Prynne was tried by the Star Chamber in 1634 and sentenced to have his ears cropped. He was also fined £5,000 and given life imprisonment. He was expelled from the Bar and from membership of the University. The book was ordered to be burned. From prison he went on issuing pamphlets attacking the bishops and the government of Charles I and once more found himself on trial before the Star Chamber, this time with the Reverend Henry Burton and Dr John Bastwick. This was in 1637, the year of *Lycidas.*

Burton (1578–1648), rector of a City of London church, was charged with sedition for two sermons he preached on 5 November 1636 and then published. He charged the bishops with trying to introduce popery into England. Bastwick (1593–1654) was already serving a prison sentence for attacking the bishops in Latin pamphlets, one of which was called *Flagellum Pontificis,* a 'whip for the bishops'. (Both Prynne and Bastwick evidently see themselves as castigators, emulating Christ in whipping out the ungodly.) In

1637 Bastwick was standing trial for attacking Laud in *The Letany of John Bastwick*. Like Prynne, he had sent his pamphlet clandestinely out from gaol.

The three were sentenced to lose their ears in the Palace Yard at Westminster, fined £5,000 each and condemned to life imprisonment, while Prynne was to be branded on each cheek with the letters 'S' and 'L' for 'seditious libeller' (see Anthology, extract 25). The sentences were regarded as outrageous because the prisoners were professional men, respectable and learned. In one of his statements to the Court, Bastwick said, '... hear my answer read, which here I tender upon the word and oath of a soldier, a gentleman, a physician' (*A Brief Relation,* page 17; *Somers Tracts,* Volume IV).

If Prynne comes over as prolix and something of a tub-thumper, Bastwick seems quite different. He is humorous, satirical, lively, and popular. Lilburne described *The Letany* as 'all full of wit', suggesting both humour, knowledge and a certain intelligent detachment. *The Letany* takes the form of a collection of items, including a letter to a friend and a mock plea to Laud for clemency, which is really another attack on episcopacy.

EXERCISE

Read the passage in the Anthology (extract 24) describing the ceremonial surrounding Laud, then consider the following questions.

What do you take to be the main drift of the argument?

What are the underlying assumptions about the ways in which leaders of the Church should behave?

What do you think is the significance of the two final sentences of the passage?

Describe the main features of the writing.

DISCUSSION

Bastwick attacks Laud for his arrogance, for his ostentatious display of wealth and for the bullying of ordinary people by his attendants. He suggests that it is scandalous that the Archbishop should seem to be setting himself up above even the King and the royal family. Bastwick's underlying assumption is that the King as the head of the Church is not in any way subordinate to an Archbishop, who as a priest should be 'meek, humble and grave'.

The description of the show of power as Laud progresses from the Star Chamber stresses the awe and respect by which he is surrounded (notice the force of words like 'pomp', 'grandeur', 'magnificence', 'multitude'), but it is immediately undermined by the vulgar, mock naïve assumption that the attendants are carrying Laud's train, which he calls his 'tail', 'for the better breaking and venting of his wind, and easing of his holy body (for it is full of holes)' – notice the pun!

He repeats the idea that the King himself is not so proud and certainly not as brutal to the people as Laud who, Bastwick claims, behaves like this all the time – it is his 'ordinary deportment'. In the last two sentences Bastwick is clearly trying to isolate the Archbishop from the King, praising Charles in order to discredit Laud and so winning a hearing from those opposed to the bishops and those loyal to the monarchy and seeking to drive a wedge between church and secular rulers. Notice the balanced contrasts in 'you would think it were the King himself, if you saw not the priest', and between 'some mighty proud Nimrod, or some furious Jehu' and 'a meek, humble and grave priest'.

There is a distinctly dramatic quality about the passage and Bastwick, you may have remarked, uses theatrical terms like 'spectacle', 'business', 'actions'; we have the call of the attendants, 'Room, room, my lord's grace is coming', and the exclamations of the costermongers, 'Save my puddings, save my codlings for the Lord's sake', with their humble concerns and reference to a different 'Lord'. There is the impression of a lot of activity in

THE LETANY

OF

JOHN BASTVVICK,

Doctor of Phisicke,

Being now full of Devotion, as well in refpect of the
common calamities of plague and peftilence; as alfo
of his owne patticular miferie: lying at this inftant in *Limbo*
Patrum. Set downe in two Letters to Mr. *Aquila Wykes,*
keeper of the Gatehoufe, his good Angell.

IN WHICH

There is an univerfall challenge to the vvhole World,
to prove the parity of Minifters, to be *jure divino.*

ALSO

A full demonftration, that the Bifhops are neither Chrifts, nor the Apoftles
Succeffors, but enemies of *Chrift* and his *Kingdome*, and of the *Kings*
moft excellent Majefties prerogative Royall.

All which hee undertaketh to make good before King and Counfell, with the
hazard of otherwife being made a prey to their infatiable indignation.

A Booke very ufefull, and profitable for all good Chriftians to read, for the
ftirring up of devotion in them likewife.

PROVERB. Chap. 25. verf. 2.

It is the glory of God to conceale a thing, but the honour of the King is to fearch
out a matter.

PRINTED

By the fpeciall procurement, and for the efpeciall ufe of our Englifh Prelats
in the yeare of Remembrance, *Anno* 1637.

Figure 2   Title page of The Letany of John Bastwick, *1637. (Bodleian Library,*
Oxford. B.7.3 Linc.)

the succession of verbs in the present tense: 'going', 'calling', 'tumbling
down', 'thrusting aside', 'flinging and tossing'. Notice the personal voice of
the writer in 'I say, you would think' and the conceding of his own response
to the scene which includes anger, pity and amusement. The tone is a mixture of idiomatic and literary: 'one can scarce keep from laughter' or 'swim-
ming like frogs about the Thames', and 'the diversity of all men's discourses'
or 'the ordinary deportment of the prelate' and the uneasy coinage 'seriosity'.
He reinforces the description by the use of groups of near synonyms, 'pomp,
grandeur, magnificence', 'wailing, mourning, and lamentation', 'pride,
arrogancy, barbarousness, and cruelty', which gives a richness of impression
and heavy emphasis.

The sentence structure is simple with a steady progression through the
events established by a succession of clauses, each giving us a picture of one
or other element in the scene.

From *A Brief Relation,* an eye-witness account of the scene as the sentences
were carried out on Prynne, Burton and Bastwick, we can sense how the

prisoners turned the occasion to their own advantage. Each spoke to the crowd declaring his willingness to undergo Christian martyrdom to break the bishops' power. They warned about the danger to English liberties and the need to defend them. Prynne challenged bishops and lawyers to open debate, while Bastwick reminded the people of the power of the press, now denied to them: '. . . but if the presses were as open to us, as formerly they have been, we should shatter his [Laud's] kingdom about his ears'. In characteristically earthy style he has just described books supporting bishops as 'full of lies, as dogs be full of fleas'. *A Brief Relation* is sympathetic to the three but seems not to exaggerate the impact of their case on the public. A newsletter of 1637 describes how, as Bastwick 'came from the gatehouse, the light common people strewed herbs and flowers before him'.

> The humours of the people were various, some wept, some laughed, and some were very reserved. I hear of a popish fellow that told some of them which wept that if so be they would turn catholics they need fear none of this punishment. Saturday all the town was full of it that Mr Prynne was dead, found dead upon his knees with his hands lifted up to heaven, but there was no such thing, for I hear he was not sick.'
>
> *(Documents Relating to the Proceedings against William Prynne, page 87.)*

Two weeks after these events the same newsbook reports that preparations are under way for the three to be sent to 'their several remote prisons' and that:

> There is a report abroad in the town that the Minister of Shoreditch, observing the humours of the people so much to compassionate these three delinquents, should deliver his sermon that they all incurred damnation which thought well of these three, who had been justly punished for their demerits. This doctrine made divers go out of the church, for the common people are extremely compassionate towards them.'
>
> (Ibid., page 91.)

That this popularity persisted can be seen from the description in Anthology extract 30.

How did men like these find the courage to risk severe punishment? The brief quotations set out below are taken from works by Prynne, Bastwick and by John Lilburne, whose first punishment was to be flogged through the streets for distributing seditious pamphlets, probably Bastwick's. (For a discussion of John Lilburne and the Levellers see Block 5, *Political Ideas.*)

EXERCISE

Read through the extracts and then jot down one or two sentences about the content of each one and what they might tell us about the psychology of their writers.

A   It being one chief article of my belief, ever since I first read the Scriptures and Tullies' Offices, that I was principally born for my country's good (next to God's glory involved in it); upon which ground I have ever bent all my studies to promote it what I might, though to my particular loss and disadvantage.

      (William Prynne, *The Epistle Dedicatory to the Sovreign Power of Parliaments and Kings,* 1643. 'Tullies' was Marcus Tullius Cicero; *The Offices* was a work of moral philosophy.)

B   . . . and if I chance to suffer any future hard measure, of what kind soever, for doing my country or Your Honours the best and faithfullest service I am able, I shall repute it my greatest honour, my chiefest

felicity, and cheerfully undergo it (through God's assistance) not as a
cross of infamy, but a crown of glory.

(Ibid.)

C   I began then exceedingly to rejoice at mine own condition, and to
think it none of the smallest beatitudes in this life to meet with
adversities, and to be confined to solitude in the midst of peril.

(John Bastwick, *The Letany of John Bastwick*, 1637; *The Somers Tracts*,
Volume V.)

D   If I die in that battle, so much the sooner I shall be sent in a chariot of
triumph to heaven; and when I come there, I will, with those that are
under the altar, cry, How long, Lord, holy and true, dost thou not
judge and avenge our blood upon them that dwell upon the earth.
And I shall with joy then and alacrity appear before that great tri-
bunal, when such judges as put me into your keeping shall wish the
mountains and rocks to fall upon them, and the hills to cover them
from the sight and presence of the Lamb that sits upon the throne, for
their impious dealing.

(Ibid.)

E   But I must confess, if I had had no more but my own natural
strength, I had sunk under the burden of my punishment, for to the
flesh the pain was very grievous and heavy: but my God in whom I
did trust was higher and stronger than myself, who strengthened and
enabled me not only to undergo the punishment with cheerfulness,
but made me triumph and with a holy disdain to insult over my
torments.

(John Lilburne, *A Work of the Beast; Tracts on Liberty*, page 6.)

F   I stand here in the place of ignominy and shame, yet to me it is not
so, but I own and embrace it, as the welcome cross of Christ, and as a
badge of my Christian profession.

(Ibid., page 9.)

G   . . . yet as I have the assurance of God in my own conscience, that in the
day of the Lord I shall be found to have been faithful . . . a time will
come when those that are now apt to censure me of rashness and
turbulency of spirit, will dearly repent that they ever admitted such a
thought, confess they have done me wrong and wish with all their
hearts they had been all of my judgement and resolution.

(John Lilburne, *The Just Defence; The Leveller Tracts*, page 453.)

DISCUSSION

All three men were deeply influenced by Foxe's *Book of Martyrs* and see
themselves as martyrs. They are sustained by the belief that they are God's
chosen instruments, and, in the case of Bastwick and Lilburne, that God will
wreak vengeance on their persecutors. It seems to have been this conviction
that they had been chosen and that there was the certainty of salvation after
death, that helped them to face the most severe physical suffering and the
psychological effects of isolation in prison. The suffering they endured was
seen by them as proof that they were indeed God's instruments.

Milton was another seventeenth-century writer who had this sense of being
God's instrument; he believed that it was through some great work of litera-
ture that he would fulfil God's intentions towards him (see 'Sonnet VII'; *The
Reason of Church Government Urged against Prelaty*; and the *Milton Study
Guide*). Such men were deeply concerned about their spiritual fitness to do
God's work – their state of grace. Many subjected themselves to keen obser-

vation of their inner emotional and spiritual states, which they recorded in diaries – a kind of spiritual balance-sheet keeping. William Haller suggests that such diaries were an equivalent of confession. Propagandists, as the short passages from Prynne, Bastwick and Lilburne show, actually published their 'balance-sheets' for all to read. Instruments of God they surely did feel themselves to be, but they also seem to have had a powerful sense of the drama of their personal circumstances and to be expressing too their sense of re-creating themselves in order to participate in the profound re-shaping of history that was going forward. This emerging concern with the psychological life of the ordinary individual in the conditions of contemporary social life was to form a significant aspect of the new literary form of the next century, the realistic novel.

We can also see in these extracts parallels with the image in John Bunyan's *The Pilgrim's Progress* (published 1678) of life as a continuous trial, a spiritual testing ground to qualify people to enter the Kingdom of Heaven. The militant Puritan set out on the pilgrimage of life embracing suffering and facing severe physical and moral tests, struggling against sin and his own weakness, just as Christian does on his journey to the Celestial City. Bunyan, like these early pamphlet writers, challenged an authoritarian church and state which threatened him with very severe punishment. He too stood trial (Radio Programme 14, *The Trials of John Bunyan*) and he wrote a spiritual autobiography, *Grace Abounding*. We know that Foxe's *Book of Martyrs* was very precious to him. His beliefs, his reading, his experience of spiritual and moral struggle and persecution come to us, transformed into great art, in the allegorical novel. (Bunyan is discussed in more detail in Block 9, *Restoration Culture*.)

One of the outstanding opposition writers of the sixteen-forties and fifties was Gerrard Winstanley. This great writer produced by the Digger movement (a fore-runner of communism in English political theory and which is discussed in Block 5, *Political Ideas*) thought and wrote deeply and creatively about class society, private ownership of the means of production, the nature of the state and what a just society should be like. He also described the psychological effects on individuals of oppression and exploitation, and his own feelings of acute social isolation.

EXERCISE

Turn to your Anthology and read the following extracts by Winstanley: extract 95, 'From *Several Pieces Gathered into One Volume*'; extract 96, 'From *Fire in the Bush*'; and extract 97, *The Epistle to Oliver Cromwell*, the section beginning 'Thus, Sir, I have reckoned up', to 'and do quiet my own spirit', page 197. What motivates Winstanley to write? What do the passages show about his state of mind? Describe the main features of his style.

DISCUSSION

Like the writers discussed above, Winstanley explains that the sense of divine guidance upholds him in adversity and that God speaks through him. There is an introspective quality about the first two passages in which he quietly reveals his inner feelings to the reader: 'my heart hath been full of deadness and uncomfortableness' and 'I have been secretly sorry' . There are convincing details, like the indication of the intensity of the cold – 'I was so stark with cold that I was forced to rise by degrees and hold by the table' – or the quick glimpse of the household incident of his leaving his friends at the table during the meal. The simple simile of the man wading 'in the dark and slabby weather' (life as a journey!) is suddenly followed by the lyrical phrase 'peace, light, life and fulness' (note the repeated 'l' sound which is reinforced by the use of 'revealed') with its suggestion of sudden surprise and of divine revelation. The same quietly lyrical quality comes at the end with the brief prayer–like exclamation.

While also introspective, the extract from *Fire in the Bush* reflects by contrast a tone of deep despair. The discussion between 'the soul' and

THE
Law of Freedom
IN A
PLATFORM:
Or, True
Magiſtracy Reſtored.

Humbly preſented to *Oliver Cromwel*, General of the Common-wealths Army in England. And to all Engliſh-men my brethren whether in Church-fellowſhip, or not in Church-fellowſhip, both ſorts walking as they conceive according to the Order of the Goſpel: and from them to all the Nations in the World.

Wherein is Declared, What is Kingly Government, and what is Commonwealths Government.

By *Jerrard Winſtanley*.

In thee, O England, is the Law ariſing up to ſhine,
If thou receive and practiſe it, the crown it wil be thine.
If thou reject, and ſtil remain a froward Son to be,
Another Land wil it receive, and take the crown from thee.
Revel. 11. 15. ———— Dan. 7. 27.

LONDON,
Printed by *J. M.* for the Author, and are to be ſold by *Giles Calvert* at the black Spred-Eagle at the Weſt end of *Pauls.* 1652.

Figure 3   Title page of Gerrard Winstanley's The Law of Freedom, 1652. *(Guildhall Library, City of London.)*

Thus Sir, I have reckoned up ſome of thoſe burdens which the people groan under.

And I being ſenſible hereof was moved in my ſelf, to preſent this Platform of Commonwealths Government unto you, wherein I have declared a full Commonwealths Freedome, according to the Rule of Righteouſneſs, which is Gods Word. It was intended for your view above two years ago, but the diſorder of the Times cauſed me to lay it aſide, with a thought never to bring it to light, &c. Likewiſe I hearing that M. *Peters* and ſome others Propounded this requeſt, That the Word of God might be conſulted with to finde out a healing Government, which I liked well, and waited to ſee ſuch a Rule come forth, for there are good rules in the Scripture if they were obeyed and practiſed: thereupon

I laid aſide this in ſilence, and ſaid, I would not make it publick; but this word was like fire in my bones ever and anon, *Thou ſhalt not bury thy talent in the earth,* therefore I was ſtirred up to give it a reſurrection, and to pick together as many of my ſcattered papers as I could finde, and to compile them into this method, which I do here preſent to you, and do quiet my own ſpirit.

Figure 4   Section from 'The Epistle Dedicatory' of The Law of Freedom, 1652. *(Guildhall Library, City of London.)*

'imaginary fear' represents the ebb and flow of Winstanley's inner debate in the face of the desertion of friends and of ostracism. One after the other short phrases, each depicting a sorrowful or suffering state, combine to create an overwhelming picture of dejection and misery. This picture is emphasized by the frequent repetition of 'thou' and 'thee' and 'thy', for example, in 'And wilt thou be alone? Yea, thou art alone . . . '. The lamentation in the second section of the extract achieves intensity by the repetition of 'I' and of the sounds ('d' and 'w'); for example, in 'I would I had died in the womb' and by the exclamatory effect of 'a bird, or beast, or some other creature' echoed in the next sentence in 'I could live, I had friends I had peace'. The paragraph closes with the despairing paradox of 'righteousness' and 'miserable wretch'.

In Winstanley's early pamphlets the Scriptures represented a major source of authority, as they did for most polemicists. Paradoxically, the continual appeal to the Scriptures as validation for diverse and opposing points of view served, in the end, to undermine their hitherto infallible position.

The Epistle to Oliver Cromwell, a kind of preface for *The Law of Freedom* (1652), stresses the importance of the Scriptures as a source of guidance and truth, though Winstanley was moving to an increasingly secular position himself, developing the view that the Bible must be understood in the light of reason and individual experience. The passage moves from a cool, practical tone, explaining the circumstances in which he comes to be offering the pamphlet, to a more intense, personal mood touching again on the theme of the power of his conscience with its simile 'like fire in my bones' and the Biblical quotation. Winstanley moves us along with the rise and fall of his own feelings, from 'silence' to 'stirred up to give it a resurrection', to the activity of compiling the 'scattered papers', and then, after presenting them, to the feeling of calm and a satisfied conscience and 'do quiet my own spirit'.

In Winstanley's earlier work there are powerful echoes of the cadences and imagery of the Bible; it is in these writings that he often claims mystical insights and inspiration. This short passage from *Truth Lifting up its Head above Scandals* (1648) gives an example of Biblical stylistic influence: 'And he shall fill the earth with himself as a corn of wheat multiplying every year fills the earth with that grain, so that all live in the light, and strength of pure reason.' (*Works of Gerrard Winstanley,* page 121.) For Winstanley, as for Milton, light is equated with truth, reason, knowledge and divine goodness.

EXERCISE

Read through the passages below and make short notes about their outstanding features.

> But now the declaration of the spirit, being but words gone out of the mouth, may be, and daily are, corrupted by the subtlety of imaginary flesh; it is the spirit within every man that tries all things; words cannot try all things: he that speaks from the flesh; shall of the flesh reap corruption; shall taste of misery that flesh brings upon himself; but he that speaks from the spirit shall of the spirit reap life: or he that preaches the Gospel, shall live of the Gospel; that is, he that speaks from the spirit shall have inward peace, life, and liberty from the spirit in the midst of all worldly straits, he shall not want life and peace within.
>
> (*Truth Lifting Up Its Head;* ibid, page 101.)

(The second passage describes the coming of a new and just society based on common ownership of the land and means of production.)

> He will throw down the mountains of the flesh, fill up the low valleys of the spirit, he will make rough ways smooth, and crooked ways straight, he will make the earth fruitful, and the winds and the

>   weather seasonable; he will throw all the powers of the earth at your
>   feet, and himself will be your governor and teacher . . .
>   *(The New Law of Righteousness,* 1649; ibid., page 153.)

DISCUSSION

In the first passage, with its reference to Galatians 6:8, there is elaborate interplay of repetition and contrast. The antithesis between 'flesh' and 'spirit', which forms the theme of the passage, is established by the very frequent repetition of the two contrasting words. This repetition is reinforced by the balance between 'reap corruption' and 'reap life', and by repetitions like 'preaches the Gospel, shall live of the Gospel'. The emphasis in the conclusion is produced by the repetition of 'peace' and 'life' and by the force of the last word 'within', which is the key to the whole passage, with the stress on the inward life and how it is to be achieved.

The second passage, echoing Isaiah 40:4, similarly exploits contrasting meanings – 'throw down', 'fill up', 'rough', 'smooth', 'crooked', 'straight' – with repetitions like 'he will throw' and 'he will make' in statements of similar length and grammatical construction. Intensity is achieved through this rhythmic interweaving of contrast and repetition.

Bastwick's description of Laud's progress, which we discussed above, provides an example of the way popular writers used theatrical conventions for immediacy and vividness. In his turn Winstanley constructs imaginary dialogues which probably reflect both theatrical convention and his experience of the meetings of sects where the members earnestly tried to elicit truth through discussion and debate. In *The Epistle to Cromwell* he presents his arguments largely in the form of a debate or in dialogue; he anticipates questions Cromwell might put to him and intersperses these with the voice of the people expressing their discontents and uneasiness.

>   It may be you will say to me, 'What shall I do?' I answer, 'You
>   are in place and power to see all burdens taken off from your friends,
>   the commoners of England.' You will say, 'What are those bur-
>   dens?'. . .
>   Most people cry, 'We have paid taxes, given free-quarter,
>   wasted our estates and lost our friends in the wars, and the taskmas-
>   ters multiply over us more than formerly.' I have asked divers this
>   question, 'Why do you say so?'
>   (Anthology, extract 97)

In *Truth Lifting Up Its Head* we have the sort of question Christian might well have put to a companion on the journey, and the idiomatic expression Bunyan might have used.

>   Q What is it to live in the Spirit?
>   A. When Flesh is made to see . . . And not led away like a bear by
>   the nose, by every object before his eyes, which the flesh lusts
>   after to enjoy. . .
>   *(Works of Gerrard Winstanley,* page 136.)

The influence of the theatre is seen most clearly in Richard Overton's *The Arraignment of Mr Persecution.* Arguing for toleration, Overton cast his pamphlet in the form of a court-room drama. Drawing on trials, the theatre and the familiar methods of allegory, he creates dramatic dialogue, naming his 'characters' after the political-religious principles under debate. Before the Judge, Lord Parliament, stands Mr Persecution on trial, with Mr God's Vengeance for the prosecution; for the defence are Sir Simon Synod (Simony) and Sir John (contemptuous name for a priest) Presbyter. The large cast includes Justices of the Peace called Reason, Humanity and Conformity. The jury has Mr Creation, Mr Politic-Power, Mr Liberty-of-Subject, Mr Innocent-Blood, Mr Orphan and Mr Light-of-Nature. The jury

THE
Araignement
OF Mr.
PERSECVTION

Prefented to the
CONSIDERATION OF THE HOUSE OF COMMONS,
and to all the COMMON PEOPLE of *England.*

WHEREIN HE IS INDICTED, ARAIGNED, CONVICTED, AND
Condemned of *emnity againſt God, and all Goodneſſe, of Treaſons, Rebellion,
Bloodſhed, &c.* and ſent to the place of *Execution.*

In the proſecution whereof, the Ieſuiticall Deſignes, *and* ſecret Encroachments *of his Defendants,* Sir *SYMON SYNOD, and the IOHN of all Sir IOHN S,*
Sir *IOHN PRESBITER, upon the Liberty of the
Subject is* detected, *and laid open.*

By Yongue MARTIN MAR-PREIST, Son
to old MARTIN the Metropolitane.

This is Licenced, and printed according to Holy Order, but not Entered into the Stationers
Monopole.

Angliæ MARTINIS *diſce favere tuis.*

EVROPE.

Printed by *MARTIN CLAW CLERGIE,* Printer to the *Reverend
·Aſſembly of Divines* and are to be ſhould at his Shop in *Toleration Street,* at the *Signe* of the *Subjects Liberty,* right
oppoſite to *Perſecuting Court.* 1645.

Figure 5   Title page of Richard Overton's The Arraignment of Mr Persecution,
1645. (Reproduced by permission of the British Library Board.)

that the defence tries to call includes Satan, Anti-Christ, Spanish Inquisition, Scotch Government (Presbyterianism), False Prophets, Assembly of Divines and Pontifical Revenue.

EXERCISE

Read the passages from the pamphlet printed in your Anthology (extract 84) and answer the following questions.

1   What is the main aim of the prosecuting counsel, Mr God's Vengeance?

2   How do the prisoner, Mr Persecution, and his defence council, Sir Symon Synod and Sir John Presbyter, seek to discredit the witnesses against them, and how do they try to establish his innocence?

3   What is the essence of the attack made by Liberty-of-Conscience?

DISCUSSION

1   Mr God's Vengeance is seeking to show that Mr Persecution has been the cause of terrible suffering and misery. His actions are directly in opposition to Christ's message of love and the possibility of salvation for everybody. The forcing of conformity has resulted in nations divided, princes being set against their people, and families split by hatred and enmity. The central

argument is for toleration, of non-Christians as well as of different Christian sects. Reason, patience and the free exchange of views are seen as the way through which God's truth will be found by everybody, and everybody may be saved. The final section of the speech refers directly to England and the effects of persecution and of attempts to impose conformity. A further aim, not shown by these passages, is to establish that Mr Persecution has a long ancestry from Popery and the Inquisition, through to Presbyterianism. (See Milton's sonnet, 'On the New Forcers of Conscience Under The Long Parliament', *The Portable Milton,* page 221.)

2 The defence try to discredit Mr God's Vengeance and his witnesses by stressing their low social origins. Christian, is attacked as a rascal, a vagrant, a person paying no tithes, an 'Anabaptist and a tubpreacher'. They stress the respectability of the prisoner, who may be defended by the authority of established precedent derived from 'The most eminent emperors, princes, councils, parliaments, etc.'

3 Liberty-of-Conscience accuses the Presbyterians of greed, for tithes in particular, which, they believed, should be upheld by the law and imposed on everybody.

The pamphlet was published without licence; instead of Overton's name and the printer's and bookseller's attribution appearing on the frontispiece, we have an author called Young Martin Mar-Priest, son of old Martin the Metropolitane, and 'printed by Martin Claw-Clergy, Printer to the Reverend Assembly of Divines, and are to be sold at his shop in Toleration Street, at the Sign of the Subjects Liberty, right opposite to Persecuting Court, 1645'. The author's attribution refers to the famous Elizabethan pamphlet writer who also attacked bishops, Martin Marprelate (a nom de plume); he seems also to have been a strong influence on Bastwick's popular satirical style.

Mr Persecution is condemned to 'return to the place from whence thou camest', (as rogues and vagabonds were sent to their parish of origin in real life), and on the Day of Judgement he is to be cast with Sir Symon and Sir John 'into the lake of fire and brimstone, where the beast and the false prophet are, there to be tormented day and night for ever and ever'.

The court scene is in the tradition which Bunyan followed in *The Pilgrim's Progress* for the trial in Vanity Fair. In 1645 it was possible for Overton to propose victory for Mr God's Vengeance, Gaffer Christian, Gaffer Liberty-of-Conscience and the rest who stood for toleration and liberty. In Bunyan, victory goes to the persecutors, the wicked and unrighteous in this world.

These opposition pamphlets, written in an urgent and energetic prose by men deeply committed to a radical cause, seek a direct way into the mind and heart of the reader. Both their message and their style were felt as a threat to stability, peace and good order after the Restoration which knew their strong commitment as 'enthusiasm'. With the Restoration the search in art as in life was one for balance, control and objectivity; aesthetic principles were being brought into closer conformity with predominant social, religious, political and philosophical values.

References

S. R. Gardiner (ed.), *Documents relating to the Proceedings against William Prynne in 1634 and 1637,* Camden Society, 1877.

W. Haller (ed.), *Tracts on Liberty in the Puritan Revolution,* New York, 1934.

W. Haller and G. Davies (eds.), *The Leveller Tracts, 1647–1653,* Columbia University Press, 1944.

C. H. Sabine (ed.) *Works of Gerrard Winstanley,* Cornell University Press, 1941.

The Somers Tracts, Volume IV, 1809; Volume V, 1811.

3 Later Seventeenth-century Prose

The search for firm social and political values mentioned by Joan Bellamy at the end of the preceding section is clearly visible in the work of Thomas Hobbes (1588–1679). Hobbes's belief that it was possible to establish philosophy on as firm a base as geometry led him to demand a prose which was as unambiguous as the geometric figures of Euclid. This desire for precision should remind you of Bacon's need for such pure and exact writing, and, indeed, Bacon had gone a long way, though more in theory than in actual practice, to make a plain prose style respectable. Plain, straightforward prose had, of course, always been around. You can find it in Anglo-Saxon and medieval times, you can find in in the overwhelming majority of private letters and journals (see excerpts from Jocelyn's Diary in the Anthology, extract 61). You can find it in Bunyan and in political pamphlets. What plain prose lacked was an acknowledgement that it could be used for scientific discourse and philosophy.

But Bacon and Hobbes were not asking merely for the simple sentences and vocabulary of everyday speech for, as it stood, everyday prose (with its slipshod grammar, its misuse of words and its ambiguity) was a crude and inaccurate instrument. What was needed was a prose stripped of elaboration and purified of vagueness.

EXERCISE

Now read Chapter IV, 'Of Speech' from Part I of *Leviathan* (pages 100–10). What is Hobbes's main concern here?

DISCUSSION

Here we see Hobbes's preoccupation with getting language straight and stripping it of abuses. Clearly language is highly respected by Hobbes – it can express, even discover, the truth, but only if man remembers 'what every name he uses stands for' and ensures that he places it 'accordingly'.

Given such an ideal, it's not surprising that Hobbes should be so suspicious of metaphors, for metaphors depend upon words being flexible in their meanings. No wonder Hobbes warns writers against the ambiguous use of words: '. . . or else he will find himselfe entangled in words, as a bird in lime-twiggs; the more he struggles, the more belimed'.

EXERCISE

Now read the third from last paragraph of Chapter V, 'Of Reason, and Science', which begins 'To conclude, The Light of human minds . . .' Do you notice anything about his attacks on verbal imagery and ambiguity?

DISCUSSION

Both in Chapter IV and Chapter V Hobbes uses verbal images to attack the use of verbal images! In the first we have the 'belimed bird', in the second that most traditional image of human understanding – 'light'.

We must be beware when writers like Hobbes claim they are writing, and should write, without any device (such as metaphor) which increases ambiguity. Hobbes does get trapped by the 'bird lime' of imagery, though clearly it doesn't turn *him* into a pathetic flutterer. But, given that he occasionally contradicts himself, it is still true, isn't it, that his prose does appear to be plain and straighforward?

If we remember that the style is part of the meaning, then we should not be surprised that Hobbes's prose is very much a demonstration of the steady, methodical approach he himself advocates. The style both transmits the meaning and shows it in action. The prose both preaches and practises.

With Hobbes, we leave the Senecan loose style and are confronted by 'plain' prose. Now, loose and plain styles clearly have a lot in common and, in fact, finally shade into one another. However, we can distinguish between them by saying that the loose style, unlike the plain, was still very conscious of its classical origins: it tended to use many latinate words and very elaborate imagery which was often sustained and developed in a way not unlike a metaphysical conceit.

EXERCISE

How revolutionary was the plain prose that Hobbes was arguing for?

DISCUSSION

In one sense it was not revolutionary at all. There was a long tradition of writing certain forms of prose plainly which stretched right back to Anglo-Saxon times. This tradition is best seen in the various English translations of the Bible from Tyndale's *New Testament* (1526) to the *Authorized Version* (1611). Most of these followed the relative simplicity of the original Hebrew and Greek texts and used a robust prose of simple and co-ordinated sentences. As the Bible was probably the most widely distributed and best known of all prose works, its style must have heavily reinforced the claims of plain prose. Important, too, was a tradition of writing plain sermons that had been established by the end of the sixteenth century. The plain sermon was predominantly, though not exclusively, the product of Puritan preachers, and could be set against the High Anglican, or 'Laudian', tradition of Andrewes and Donne. (This distinction is discussed in Block 2, *A Changing Culture.*)

In many handbooks dealing with the writing of sermons, plain preachers vehemently argued the essentially moral (rather than stylistic) justification for plain prose. John Wilkins (1614–72) in *Ecclesiastes* (1646) puts the case forceably:

> Obscurity in the discourse is an argument of ignorance in the mind. The greatest learning is to be seen in the greatest plainness. The more clearly we understand anything ourselves, the more easily can we expound it to others . . . And it will not become the Majesty of a Divine Embassage to be garnished out with flaunting affected Eloquence. How unsuitable is it to the expectation of a hungry soul who comes unto this ordinance with a desire of spiritual comfort and instruction, and there to hear only a starched speech full of puerile worded Rhetorik?

Figure 6   Detail of portrait of Bishop Thomas Sprat by Michael Dahl, c. 1712. Sprat became Bishop of Rochester in 1684. (Bodleian Library, Oxford.)

Here obscurity is identified with ignorance and learning with plainness in a way which would have been thoroughly approved of by Hobbes. So, in many ways plain prose was traditional not novel.

But there were two ways in which Hobbes *was* being revolutionary. Plain prose was used mostly in popular literature (the majority of sermons could be classified under this head). What Hobbes was suggesting was that learned prose should be plain – that certainly was new. Revolutionary, too, was the severity of his plainness.

The scientists and philosophers of the newly formed Royal Society (established 1662) felt equally committed to a plain style, though most of them were strongly opposed to Hobbes's philosophy. Experimental science had been rising in intellectual status and importance ever since Bacon, and had finally 'arrived' with the creation of the Royal Society. As the new science rose, so did the 'old science', based upon the teachings of Aristotle and his medieval interpreters, go into a decline. Such 'old science' was still taught at the universities and was, at least in the minds of the new scientists, closely identified with the rhetorical language used for dispute in those universities. (For a discussion of university education in the mid-seventeenth century see Block 4, *The Revolution and its Impact*). Thus such complex language became identified with discredited theories. Indeed, it was seen as being responsible for such theories: if men had not used such bafflingly complicated sentences with so many obscure words, the intellectual poverty of Aristotelian theory would have been seen ages ago – and challenged. Elaborate language had been used to bamboozle and confuse – it had told lies. So to write plain English was not just a useful way of presenting scientific values unambiguously – it was a moral duty. Plainness became synonymous with truth, complexity with untruth. To adorn was to disguise. What was wanted was the naked truth, nakedly expressed.

EXERCISE

Thomas Sprat (1635–1713), Bishop of Rochester and first historian of the Royal Society, provides us with one of the most articulate versions of this argument. Please read the paragraph by Sprat at the beginning of Section 1 and the passage below; both are from his *History of the Royal Society* (1667).

> . . . a constant resolution, to reject all the amplifications, digressions, and swellings of style: to return back to the primitive purity, and shortness, when men delivered so many things, almost in an equal number of words. They have exacted from all their members, a close, naked, natural way of speaking; positive expressions; clear senses; a native easiness: bringing all things as near the mathematical plainness as they can; and preferring the language of artizans, countrymen, and merchants, before that, of wits or scholars.

Sprat is making a number of points about the social significance of language. See if you can jot one or two down before reading further.

DISCUSSION

In the first paragraph Sprat attacks 'eloquence', that is, anything other than plain prose, as being something that is troublesome and rude, something almost non-U.

In the second paragraph he advocates a style which is 'natural', 'easy', 'clear', and corresponds to the speech of common man in society, the language of 'artizans, countrymen, and merchants', rather than the discourse of court or university.

In fact the plain style of the Royal Society has three separate but interlinked justifications:

Intellectual: Straightforward, unambiguous language is needed for the exact recording of scientific data.

Moral: Complexity is a way of lying, plain words reveal the naked truth.

Social: A rejection of the language of a narrow clique, in favour of the speech of common man.

Did you notice in Sprat's second paragraph a number of hints about what he thought of the original nature of language? Sprat talks about 'primitive purity, and shortness', a time when 'men delivered so many things, almost in an equal number of words'. It's a vision of linguistic innocence. With such an ideal the complication of language must have seemed to Sprat and his colleagues the equivalent of the Fall of Man. Indeed Bacon had made a similar point, using the same Biblical reference, in his *Great Instauration* (1620): '. . . to set everything forth, as far as may be, plainly and perspicuously (for nakedness of the man is still, as nakedness of the body once was, the companion of innocence and simplicity). . .'.

The fervour with which Sprat advocates plain prose is almost as religious in tone as it is in imagery. It sounds like a spiritual crusade and, in a sense, that's just what it was. It certainly gained converts as other religious crusades did, witness Joseph Glanvill (1636–80) who wrote the *Vanity of Dogmatizing* in 1661. This was a broad survey of contemporary philosophical thought expressed, at least originally, in prose not unlike Sir Thomas Browne's (see Anthology, extract 127). By 1664 Glanville had produced a second version of this work (now called *Scepsis Scientifica*) with a prefatory

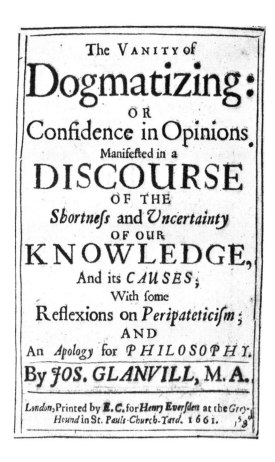

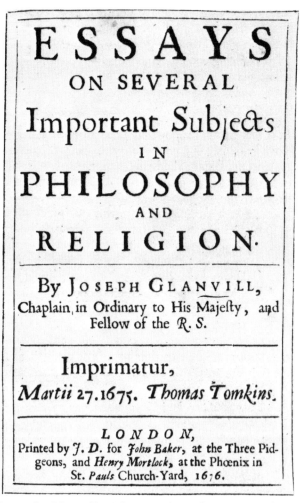

Figure 7 (left)   Title page of Joseph Glanvill's The Vanity of Dogmatizing, *1661. (Bodleian Library, Oxford. Wood 127(2).)*

Figure 8 (right)   Title page of Joseph Glanvill's Essays on Several Important Subjects in Philosophy and Religion, *1676. Note how, in comparison with* The Vanity of Dogmatizing, *the greater simplicity of the typography and layout of the title page reflects the change to a plain prose style. (Bodleian Library, Oxford. 40P. 52(4).)*

address celebrating the Royal Society. In the same year Glanvill became a member of the Society. In 1676 he re-issued the work in a highly condensed and almost wholly rewritten form as the first essay in his *Essays on Several Important Subjects in Philosophy and Religion*. Notice the change in title from the grand (*Vanity of Dogmatizing*), through the scholarly (*Scepsis Scientifica*) to the ploddingly honest (*Essays*).

Let's compare the prose of the first and third editions.

1661	*1676*
If we will take the literal evidence of our Eyes: the Aethereal Coal moves no more than this Inferior clod doth.	To Sense the Sun stands still also; and no Eye can perceive its Actual motion.

Note that 'Aethereal Coal' becomes the 'Sun'; 'Inferior clod' (the earth) disappears. 'The literal evidence of our Eyes' condenses into 'Sense' and 'perceive', and 'we' and 'our', which involve the reader, become the impersonal 'no Eye'.

The legitimizing of plain prose reflects a fundamental shift in the way man looked at the world. The complex prose of Andrewes and Donne in part reflects their sense of the complexity even, perhaps, of the final incomprehensibility of the world. With the 'plain' sermon and, above all, with the calm prose of the Royal Society, things are different. Its relative simplicity expresses a new attitude to a world which is now seen as basically simple and clear in its workings. Such a world *could* be fully understood, but only if writers rejected both the excesses of Senecan and the enthusiasms of Puritan prose and stuck to a middle course with a moderate style.

EXERCISE

The last writer I want to look at is John Dryden (1631–1700). Please read the excerpt from Dryden's Preface to the *Aeneid* in the Anthology, extract 135. Jot down any features of Dryden's style which strike you as odd or interesting.

DISCUSSION

In a sense this was a trick question because my answer would have to be: no, there is nothing particularly odd or unusual about Dryden's prose. It is plain but not too plain, for Dryden is quite capable of using imagery though, unlike Donne's, it tends to do one job and then be discarded. Although there is some subordination, many of his sentences are relatively simple in structure. There is the use of repetition to reinforce a point, but with none of the accelerating significance evident in, say, Donne's insistent repetition. There is the occasional use of aphorism: 'we are naturally prone to imitate what we admire'. Dryden's style can be punchy when it wants to be, witness the neat image of the mermaid to summarize the danger and ultimate disappointment of the unnatural: 'the fine woman ends in a fish's tail'. But many of its punches are deliberately pulled, indeed it seems almost determined not to draw attention to itself as a style.

For many late seventeenth-century writers good writing became part of good manners. And it was not good manners to baffle and confuse your reader with hard words or complex sentences. A gentleman writer would have, to use Sprat's words, '. . . a close, naked, natural way of speaking . . . a native easiness'. To an extent this emphasis on open, clear prose was determined by the imagined audience for that prose, because a gentleman's behaviour would naturally be appropriate to the company he kept. This imagined audience was no longer felt to be just a highly educated clique of courtiers, Inns of Court and university wits who would have appreciated a sermon by Andrewes or Donne. We don't need to take Sprat's claim literally (that the language to be used now was that of 'artizans, countrymen and merchants') to sense that the new market for 'serious' prose was the broad mass of the unscholarly but well-educated. The attitude to this new audience was new, too. They were neither to be preached at nor displayed to, but were to be talked *with*. Hence much of Dryden's prose is 'conversational' in tone.

Dryden's prose can be seen as a compromise, steering its way between the absolute bareness of the Royal Society ideal and the excesses of Andrewes and Donne. It is a style which, because it does not have a pronounced character, is much more flexible than most of the other styles we have looked at; a style which, like the gentleman who wrote it, is accommodating and self-effacing.

If you were to view this final product of the many changes in seventeenth-century prose style positively, you could claim that Dryden's lucid, neutral style was a triumphant product of intellectual evolutionary forces which had selected the best elements from many earlier styles and had fused them together to produce an effective, universally intelligible English prose. In many ways you would be right. The prose that Dryden wrote is almost as accessible today as it was in 1680. Despite further changes in the eighteenth and nineteenth centuries, it was to be the twentieth century before prose was again to undergo the intensity of stylistic experiment to which it was subjected during the seventeenth century. Those challenges it did meet – the novel, the rise of journalism – it coped with well without itself being radically altered. Yet – 'neutral' is very close to 'neutered', and many would argue that, though perhaps socially inevitable, the moderate plain style of Dryden represents a sad decline from the idiosyncratic richness of an Andrewes or a Donne.

We should not end on a sad note. The language Dryden passed on to the eighteenth century was, whatever its limitations, too flexible to be inhibiting for long. If it has remained the main theme of our prose style, it has also allowed enough freedom for a whole variety of remarkable variations to be played upon it.

Further reading

John Carey, 'Sixteenth and Seventeenth Century Prose' in *English Poetry and Prose 1540–1674* (ed. C. Ricks), Sphere, 1970.

S. E. Fish (ed.), *Seventeenth Century Prose: Modern Essays in Criticism,* Oxford University Press, New York, 1971.

I. A. Gordon, *The Movement of English Prose,* Longman, 1966.

Roger Sharrock (ed.), *Pelican Book of English Prose* (Volume 1), Penguin, 1970.

B. Vickers, *Seventeenth Century Prose,* Longman, 1969.

Seventeenth-century England:
A Changing Culture, 1618–1689